COYOTES

RIO NUEVO PUBLISHERS®

P.O. Box 5250, Tucson, Arizona 85703-0250

(520) 623-9558, www.rionuevo.com

The Navajo tale "How Coyote Placed the Stars in the Sky" and the Hopi tale "Coyote and the Blue Jays" are retold here by Lauray Yule. The Zuni tale "How the Corn Pests Were Ensnared" is adapted from *Zuni Coyote Tales*, by Frank Hamilton Cushing, published by University of Arizona Press.

Cover and Interior Design: Karen Schober, Seattle, Washington

Library of Congress Cataloging-in-Publication Data

Yule, Lauray.
  Coyotes / Lauray Yule.
    p. cm. -- (Look West)
  Includes bibliographical references.
  ISBN 1-887896-60-0 (hardcover)
  1. Coyote. I. Title. II. Series.
  QL737.C22Y85 2004
  599.77'25--dc22

                                    2004005796

Printed in Hong Kong
10 9 8 7 6 5 4 3 2 1

COYOTES

Lauray Yule

LOOK WEST
SERIES

RIO NUEVO PUBLISHERS
TUCSON, ARIZONA

IT BEGINS WITH A SINGLE BARK OR TWO...

THEN...SILENCE.

SUDDENLY, THERE'S AN ANSWERING YIP...A YAP...

AND AS SUNSET FADES INTO NIGHT, A HOWL INTRODUCES A

PRIMORDIAL COYOTE SYMPHONY: SCREAMS, YIPS, YAPS,

BARKS, AND WAILS BLEND INTO EVER-CHANGING MUSIC.

NO PHRASE IS REPEATED.

Just as suddenly as it began, the symphony ends. Listeners are left with eerie echoes, and only a feeling—no understanding of the ghostly canine that sang out and took us back to a time when hunters and the hunted knew only instinctive survival. Often heard but seldom seen, the coyote today is a symbol of freedoms buried deep in our distant past.

‖ ANCIENT HISTORY ‖

Where did this resilient, clever canine, long considered an emblem of the Old West, come from?

Coyotes evolved only in the New World. Several types of dog-like predators hunted the open North American landscapes about three to twelve million years ago, including dire wolves, the largest canine that ever lived. Fossils of this 125- to 175-pound predator date back to the last Ice Age, about two to four million years ago. Dire wolves fed on large herbivores, the now-extinct predecessors of today's bison and horses.

Coyote with mange, a common disease among canids.

Meanwhile, in the shadow of dire wolves, small fox-like critters with less finicky culinary tastes evolved. They ate everything from bugs, small rodents, and reptiles, to nuts and fruit. Dire wolves, partly because they were so specialized, became extinct about 16,000 years

Coyote pups are weaned by eight weeks of age.

ago, along with their big prey. But smaller canids, the ancestors of wolves, coyotes, and foxes, endured.

The earliest fossils resembling coyotes were found in what is now Maryland and date back to the Ice Age. The North American gray wolf, *Canis lupus,* thrived across the continent for thousands of years. However, because wolves require large prey to survive, their populations declined as civilization encroached.

Coyotes and foxes, though, are thriving and have adapted to rapidly changing environments. Coyotes, in fact, have expanded their range across the continent and into Central America, including urban environments such as New York City and other large metropolitan areas.

THE "BARKING DOG"

If you search the Internet for "coyote," you'll get matches for everything from athletic teams, clothing, gourmet groceries, and liquor, to sunglasses and rock bands—more than 370,000 sites! The coyote image is popular.

If you search for *"Canis latrans,"* the match list is probably closer to five thousand. *Canis latrans* ("barking dog") is the scientific name

Fur traders display the pelts of coyotes, bobcats, and other animals.

for the coyote, also known as the prairie wolf, bush wolf, or brush wolf in parts of North America. The Latin name comes from the "yip-yap-howling" it does any time the spirit moves it: sundown or sunrise, when an airplane passes overhead, when it's trying to locate family members or hunting buddies, and—some experts think—just for the sheer joy of self-expression.

Yosemite National Park, California.

The word "coyote" dates back to the ancient Aztecs. Coyotlinauatl was an Aztec god whose faithful wore coyote skins. Aztecs also worshipped a moon goddess, Coyolxauhqui, meaning "bayer-at-the-moon." Names used by Southwestern tribes refer to coyote as "God's dog," no doubt a link to the ancient Aztec word *coyotl.*

Despite efforts by early Old West pioneers to get the common name "prairie wolf" to stick, the Aztec coyotl managed to reign as root word for today's "coyote." In the northern parts of its range, the name is pronounced KY-OAT, with the "e" silent. In the south and southwestern part of its habitat, it's "KY-OH-TEE" or "KOY-OH-TEH" (the Spanish pronunciation).

FROM A DISTANCE

Coyotes generally shy away from human encounters. Catching a glimpse of one is rare—and usually from a distance, with binoculars if you're lucky.

People often confuse coyotes with wolves, gray foxes, and even shepherd or husky-type domestic dogs, especially if the animal is making tracks to slip away. A coyote's pelt has a mixture of black, cream, gray, yellow, and rusty brown—excellent camouflage for a predator that relies on stealth to survive. Coyotes at higher elevations or latitudes tend to be darker, and those in the desert display more yellow-browns. When coyotes shed in spring and early summer, they look scruffy as their underfur sloughs off in patches. Their coats are prime and luxurious in winter and fall, trapping heat about five times better than their lightweight summer "jackets."

While they may appear larger than life at a first glance, coyotes vary in size and weight with geography. Larger, heavier animals live in northern and eastern climes (averaging about thirty-five pounds, sometimes reaching fifty). Western and Southwestern coyotes generally weigh in at twenty to twenty-five pounds. Adult animals typically stand about twenty inches tall at the shoulder and measure four feet from nose to tail tip—about the size of a small Australian shepherd. Coyotes generally have bushier tails than domestic dogs, and they carry them low when running, unlike foxes or wolves. Female coyotes are smaller than males.

FACES DON'T LIE

Perhaps no characteristic sets coyotes apart from other canids more than their distinctive facial features and markings, especially the dark-

Yellowstone National Park, Wyoming.

rimmed, golden-yellow eyes that reveal a calculating intelligence and the curiosity of a high-order predator: a coyote's stare is arresting!

Large, rust-colored pointed ears, held more erect than dogs' or wolves' ears, also add a sense of "smartness." So does a narrow, pointed nose, tapering to black nostrils. A whitish to cream-colored lower jaw blends down through the chest and belly.

Adult male coyotes have broader faces and noses than females or juveniles. Researchers use a host of terms for coyote facial expressions, including neutral, alert, low-intensity threat, aggressive threat, defensive-aggressive threat, and submissive play face. And because of the combination of jawline and coloration, an alert, relaxed adult coyote always seems to display a sly smile.

‖ BUILT TO SURVIVE ‖

As with many wild canines, a coyote's back feet are slightly larger than the front ones. They have five toes on the front feet (one is higher—called the "dew claw"), and four on the hind ones. They can cruise along at a tireless trot on those long, thin legs made for covering great distances. Keen eyes, ears, and nose remain alert for the slightest hint of prey or danger.

Yellowstone National Park, Wyoming.

Coyotes have been clocked at speeds up to forty-five miles an hour for short runs, and they swim well. They live in a range of one (if prey is plentiful) to twenty-five square miles, though their endurance is phenomenal. If times are hard, or coyotes get displaced from a home territory, they'll travel up to four hundred miles to find food.

Coyotes live about four to six years in the wild, but can reach twelve years—also the average for dogs—if they stay healthy and keep out of harm's way.

COYOTE COMMUNICATION

Do bared fangs, open mouth, a growl, and arched back mean anything to you? If you're a *Canis latrans,* it does. Coyotes communicate using a combination of sounds, facial expressions, and body language. Coyote postures falls into four broad categories, though they can change in an eye-blink. They begin posturing as pups; it establishes their status in the coyote world—usually for life.

PASSIVE-SUBMISSIVE When a pup or submissive adult rolls over on its back, belly and throat exposed, it says, "I'm helpless and no threat." The dominant coyote frequently stands over the offender, legs stiff, looking down on its "victim." All coyotes act passive-submissive at times, including when a family has regrouped after hunting. It becomes a "hi, how'd it go?" and is combined with other postures, tail wagging, groveling, licking, pawing, and lots of vocalization.

PASSIVE-AGGRESSIVE Back arched, tail tucked, with head held low and ears back, is another passive-submissive display that can become passive-aggressive if the mood changes. A truly submissive coyote's mouth is closed and hackles are down. If there's confrontation—such as competition for food—the submissive animal may raise its hackles and gape its mouth into an ingratiating, teeth-showing grin. The dominant *Canis latrans* may see this as a threat and run the other coyote off—even if it's a family member.

DEFENSIVE-THREAT When pushed to it—either by the unwanted attention of a clan mate, an intruding coyote, or a predator—*Canis latrans* shifts to a defensive-threat posture: back even further arched, legs stiff, head down with mouth gaping wide, growling, and hackles raised. Its tail is held low but not between the legs. This coyote means business.

AGGRESSIVE-THREAT Finally, if a fight appears inevitable, a coyote—usually "top dog"—uses aggressive-threat body language: back straight, tail raised, hackles up on both the shoulders and neck, legs stiff, head held high with ears forward, and a full-blown teeth-bared, growling, mouth gape.

Our first reaction may be to interpret all this submissiveness, dominance, posturing, groveling, and vocal repertoire as signs of violence. In fact, it actually helps *avoid* fighting and possible injury or death within a coyote group. Full-blown fights are rare; usually the rituals defuse conflict. Dangerous challenges arise when a strange coyote (or group of coyotes) tries to assume "squatter's rights" in a clan's territory. Even then, the established group sometimes accepts the newcomer. Other conflicts occur when one coyote tries to assume dominance over another family leader—generally the breeding male.

All in all, however, *Canis latrans* seems to have a remarkable ability to get along with fellow coyotes. That nightly concert and laughing face tell the story.

Domination and submission.

COYOTE "GHOSTS" IN SAND, MUD, AND SNOW

Considering the amazing number of places they inhabit, coyotes are some of the most elusive wild critters living shoulder-to-shoulder with humans. But we can learn more about coyote lifestyle in back yards and open spaces everywhere, because *Canis latrans* does leave signs of passage.

KNOW WHAT TO LOOK FOR Coyote tracks are quite similar to those of dogs, foxes, and bobcats, but with some subtle differences.

Coyote tracks are compact, long oval shapes, about $2\frac{1}{2}$ x $1\frac{3}{4}$ inches in size. The nails show, and distance between tracks is about 15 inches. Important clue: *Canis latrans* tends to move in a purposeful straight line, usually at a trot. Coyotes don't dither at every bush along their selected route.

Dog tracks, unlike coyote tracks, vary greatly in size and in the distance between them. Their nails show, but the toes tend to splay. One important clue: Dogs tend to meander along a route, sniffing at every scent. Sometimes dogs stumble, drag their feet, or backtrack; a coyote rarely does any of these.

Fox tracks are shaped like a coyote's: compact, long, oval, about 2 x 1½ inches in size. Since foxes weigh less than coyotes, the track leaves a "delicate" impression. Nail marks may or may not be present. Distance between tracks is about 10 inches.

Bobcat paw prints, oval or circular in shape, show no clawmarks. The tracks are about 2 x 2 inches in diameter, with a distinct small indentation at the top of the main pad below the toes. Another clue: Bobcats place the pawprints of their hind feet in the tracks of their front feet—especially when stalking prey.

KNOW WHERE TO LOOK Coyotes often travel roadways (both paved and dirt), hiking trails and other pathways, washes, and along creekbeds. They use game and stock trails, and they visit water sources.

KNOW WHEN TO LOOK Just after a rain or light snowfall is the best time to discover "ghosts" of critters passing. Snow is ideal, since the paw prints are clear, sharp and easy to identify. Mud is also excellent, while sand is trickier. Undisturbed fine dust of dirt roads and trails is good. The best time for tracking is when the sun is low on the horizon and you are facing into it so the tracks stand out through contrast.

‖ WHAT'S FOR DINNER? ‖

Coyotes eat just about anything—a principal reason they have adapted to so many environmental situations. At least 80 percent of coyote diet in any habitat is rabbits, hares (jackrabbits), mice, packrats, squirrels, voles, gophers, lizards, insects, and arthropods. (Scorpions are deftly snatched and crunched down, avoiding the tail's bulbous stinger!) Birds—particularly fallen nestlings and grounddwellers such as quail and their eggs—also make potential meals. Coyotes don't turn up their noses at carrion or roadkill. (Even porcupine is on the menu, cautiously flipped over to expose the spineless underbelly.)

Though primarily carnivores, coyotes also eat prickly pear cactus fruit, hackberries, grasses, and other wild berries and nuts, including juniper berries and piñon-pine nuts, depending on where they live.

In urbanized or agricultural country, *Canis latrans* raids poorly secured domestic-fowl pens, fruit orchards, and vegetable gardens. Pears, apples, figs, grapes, and melons—even commercial chilepepper fields aren't spared: the bandits eat the pepper flesh and spit out the seeds!

Small rodents, such as this vole, provide most of a coyote's diet.

Careless cleanup by campground or picnic-area users produces an abundance of food: a coyote learns quickly that overflowing garbage cans or poorly kept campsites offer a wide selection of delights. Streetwise urban coyotes raid trash bins. Small pets—cats and dogs—are also on *Canis latrans'* menu, and a pet-food dish left out overnight offers a midnight snack.

However, contrary to media mythology, coyotes rarely eat road-runners. There's simply not enough nourishment under those feathers to warrant a chase for a mere hors d'oeuvre.

SOCIAL INTERACTION: PUPS "RULE"

Coyote society is highly flexible. They're not loners—except at times. They don't develop long-term pair bonds—except when it's convenient. And they don't form packs—except once in a while.

However, coyote life does have a central bond: pups rule!

Within the lives of almost all high-order predators, producing offspring and rearing them to adulthood becomes a social focal point. Without a next generation, a species' survival is jeopardized. And coyotes are no exception. Their cooperation to produce the next generation of skilled survivalists has made them one of the

Pups first venture out of the den around two weeks of age.

most successful wild canids ever to trot the planet.

What could be loosely called a coyote pack, band, or clan centers on a mated pair, their current litter of pups, perhaps a couple of youngsters from previous years, and an "aunt" or "uncle" that may not even be related to the central male and female. All adults care for the current puppies, including sharing babysitting duties while others hunt.

Coyotes reach adulthood at two years. Unlike domestic dogs, both male and female coyotes come in season just once a year, in winter. When a pair breeds successfully, pups are born about sixty days later, usually in April or May. Litter size varies from one to more than ten puppies, though four to six is average.

Family groups pass coyote culture on to the next generation.

The pups come into the world as blind, helpless little brown fur-balls in an excavated den or natural hideout like a crevice in a rock-walled wash. (Coyotes often dig several dens and move the pups often. If anything threatens the babies, including a human observer, puppies are whisked to a new den.)

Pups remain underground about two weeks. Then, with eyes wide open, they tumble out of the den for play sessions. Through mock fights, tug-of-war, chase games, and worrying the ears and tails of doting adult members of the coyote band, they hone skills that create successful hunters. They now eat solid food regurgitated by adult coyotes and don't require much milk from mom.

STALK AND POUNCE

When coyote pups reach six weeks old, they stalk and pounce on insects for snacks. By seven weeks old, they might make a meal of an unwary lizard or mouse, fought over with puppy snarls. They also begin to resemble adults: noses narrow, round ears get pointy, and brown baby coats change to coyote "camo."

At nine weeks, the gangly youngsters tag after family mates on hunting expeditions, learning by example, coupled with instinct.

A pack enjoys the remains of an elk carcass in Yellowstone National Park.

By summer's end, they're on their own, though they generally stick close to the home territory until late fall—or even longer if the family group doesn't run them off. Some researchers believe *Canis latrans* extended families keep in touch with "group howls," even after young coyotes establish new territories: one coyote lets out a yip, and others—even miles away—pick up the chorus. They may rendezvous to share greetings and food.

A TYPICAL HUNT

Coyotes are most active at night and during the gray light of dawn and dusk, though daytime sightings have become more frequent throughout

their continental habitat. No matter where coyotes live, they tend to travel the route of least resistance: washes, paths, the tops of backyard walls, alleyways, and (unfortunately for the coyote at times) streets and roadways.

On a hunt, a coyote's acute senses of hearing, smell, and sight kick in. They know their territorial zones, and they'll often start at a location where small rodents—mice, gophers, ground squirrels, or packrats, even grasshoppers—offer tapas-style bites. These protein-rich morsels require minimal stalking and only a quick pounce and snap of the jaws.

A faint rustling sound or whiff of scent makes a coyote freeze and devote undivided attention to a potential meal. They'll even pause in mid-stride and "hold point" until the perfect time to move: then it may be a slow creep or a swift rush and pounce to stun prey, which is gobbled down in one or two bites.

‖ THE BUDDY SYSTEM ‖

Coyotes usually hunt alone or in pairs, rather than pack-style like wolves.

The buddy system works well: two sets of sharp eyes, ears, and noses double the chances of finding and catching prey. If a larger

Coyotes don't always hunt with the same partners, although they do have favorites.

critter such as a cottontail or jackrabbit is flushed out, a coyote pair takes turns running down the target until it's tired and confused, then one *Canis latrans* corners the prey and distracts it while its partner moves in for the kill.

Another teamwork operation involves a "you dig, I'll catch" approach, used for ground-dwelling rodents. One coyote excavates a rodent burrow while the other watches escape holes. When the sought-after critter panics and bolts, it's a quick end in a set of sharp canine teeth. Some coyote teams trade off digging and catching duties as the hunt progresses.

‖ COYOTE TALES ‖

Throughout human history, storytelling has served as a way to convey day-to-day living principles, share information, and entertain. No animal has received as much attention in Native American legend as Coyote. Seen as a creator of life, a deity, trickster (both friend and foe), gift giver, lecher, deceiver, and greedy glutton, sometimes poor Coyote is even a fool. Though the critter suffers misadventures that would kill any mortal being, Coyote never dies (at least not permanently): supreme survivor, this wild canine

THE ODD COUPLE

If you don't have a coyote hunting pal, how about a badger? Yes, it's true: somehow, once upon a time, the ingenious coyote figured out this was an advantageous match.

Typically, coyotes hook up with badgers when burrowing rodents are particularly abundant. No critter digs faster and with more determination than a badger, and while a badger digs for dinner, the alert coyote stands by, watching the access holes. When a rodent bolts, the coyote pounces, and with minimum effort, it's a meal deal.

Something must bind coyotes and badgers: this "odd couple" has been noted for centuries by Native Americans, pioneers, and modern-day observers. This strange

relationship is often helped along by the coyote "pardner." The long-legged canines sometimes "herd" their much slower, short-legged badger buddies to new, rodent-rich burrow sites.

cheats death every time, in every story told by native peoples throughout North America.

Almost all tribes—from Canada to Mexico and Central America—tell similar tales of Coyote's escapades with Rabbit, Crow, Turtle, Snake, and others, with ratings varying from "G" to "adults only." Here are three examples from Southwestern tribes.

HOW COYOTE PLACED THE STARS IN THE SKY (NAVAJO)

Long ago, before the two-legged ones walked on Earth, the world was different from how it is today. At that time, in the beginning, no stars or moon shone in the night sky. Nights were pitch black, and the animals could not see when they walked around, so they kept running into each other. They decided to go ask the Great Spirit what to do.

The animals told the Great Spirit they were happy and glad for everything they had so far, but they wanted more: They wanted to see at night. Great Spirit smiled and said, "Watch this, all of you." He took a bright, shiny pebble from a creek and put it in the sky. Lo and behold, it was a star.

"This is the star that does not move—the North Star (Polaris). You can always find it, and when you get lost, you can use it to find your way home.

"Now go and collect more shiny pebbles, put them in a bag, and carry them up to the sky to make images of yourselves," said the Great Spirit.

The animals began making their shapes in the sky with the bright pebbles. But soon, all the animals, small and large, got tired. They went back to the Great Spirit to once again ask advice. "Find Coyote," Great Spirit told them. "He will help you if you tell him to."

Coyote thought he was far superior to all other animals—more clever and wise than any of them. He didn't want to waste his time to help them. But he did not want to anger Great Spirit either. He told the animals to leave the pebbles with him, and he would finish placing their images in the sky.

When all the animals were gone, vain Coyote thought: "What a wonderful picture of *me* I will design in the sky! It will bigger, brighter, and more magnificent than any of the others!"

Coyote became impatient with placing each shiny stone just so in the sky. Besides, he didn't really care about the shapes of the other

A traditional Navajo sandpainting illustrates the myth of First Coyote stealing fire.

animals anyway. Frustrated, he finally grabbed the bag of pebbles and hurled them skyward. The stones went everywhere—all over the heavens. None of the pictures of the animals were complete—not even Coyote's.

That's why all the shapes in the sky—the constellations—don't look complete, and why some don't look anything like their namesakes. Many of the pebbles were flung in a great band across the sky—the Milky Way—and look more like a river of stars than an animal.

In the end, Coyote was punished for his dishonesty and laziness. By flinging all the stones into the sky, he had saved none for his own image. Coyote was frustrated and howled in anger.

That is why you hear Coyote howl at night: He cannot see his own image in the clear night skies.

COYOTE AND THE BLUE JAYS (HOPI)

Coyote went hunting one day to feed her many children, but her hunt was not successful. She was headed home when she came upon a flock of Blue Jays playing a game. First they flew up into the air, then they hovered, and then they landed again. Coyote was curious and trotted closer.

Now she saw that only one bird took flight at a time. When it was high in the air, the bird dropped something. Then the rest of the flock flew up and caught whatever it was. Coyote approached the birds, but to her surprise they didn't fly away. "What game is this?" she asked.

"It's the Eye Game," said the Blue Jays. "It's fun! Here's how it goes: One bird takes out an eye. Another bird takes the eye and flies way, way up in the air. Then he drops it. And then the rest of the birds carry the first bird up to catch his eye and pop it back in the socket."

"Oh, can I play too?" begged Coyote.

Mimbres Black-on-white bowl featuring a wolf or coyote design (A.D. 950–1300, southern New Mexico area).

The birds agreed. And since Coyote always wanted to be the best at everything, she took out *both* her eyes and handed them over.

Grabbing Coyote's eyes, two Blue Jays soared high into the sky. Then they let the eyes go. Down, down, down they fell. Meanwhile the birds on the ground seized Coyote and lifted her by her rear legs, her ears, her tail, and her back, but they left her front legs flapping free to catch her eyes. Up, up, up they rose.

"Watch out! Here come your eyes!" squawked the Blue Jays all together. So many loud voices all at once! They confused Coyote, and she snatched blindly at the air while her eyes fell past her to the ground.

"Where are my eyes?" cried Coyote.

The birds flew Coyote back down to earth again, but they landed far away from her eyes. "That's the end of the Eye Game, " said the Blue Jays, and they left her there alone.

Coyote hunted and hunted, fumbling and feeling her way along, but she couldn't find her eyes, and she couldn't find the way home. At last she came to a piñon pine tree, and on the ground beneath it she found some pine pitch. She filled her eye sockets with that pitch, and somehow it restored her sight, so with her new yellow eyeballs she found her way back to her children again. And that's why all coyotes have yellow eyes now.

Mayo Indian mask by Arnulfo Yocupicio and Amelia Rabago Zasueta of Sonora, Mexico, 2003.

‖ HOW THE CORN-PESTS WERE ENSNARED (ZUNI) ‖

Long ago, there lived a beautiful maiden, the daughter of a rich man. She had everything a maiden could wish for—blankets and mantles, embroidered dresses and sashes, buckskins and moccasins, turquoise earrings and shell necklaces and bracelets.

She had one problem. She had cornfields, so large that those who planted and worked them could not look after them. As soon as the corn ears became full and sweet, animals broke into the fields and ate the corn. Other pests troubled her as well: every unmarried young man in the valley was running mad over her charms. They never gave the girl peace.

She decided to put the two pests together and get rid of one or the other. When these young men were importunate, she would say to them, "Look! If you go to my cornfields and destroy or scare away the pests that eat my corn, I will marry you."

The young men tried and tried, but it was no use.

There was one young fellow who lived in one of the outer towns, the poorest among the people. Not only that, he was so ugly that no woman ever looked at him without laughing. He had bright twinkling eyes, however, and that means more than all else sometimes.

He had no present to offer the girl, but he went to her house one evening. She took the young man aside and gave him her conditions.

The next day the young man went down to her cornfield and dug a pit. Then he went to the mountain and got some thin poles. Placing them across the hole, he spread earth across them and set up cornstalks just as though no hole had been dug there. He put tempting bait over the center of these weak poles.

That night, the Coyotes began to sing, and all sorts of creatures came down from the mountain. The Coyotes reached the field first, being swift of foot, and one noticed the tempting morsels that lay over the hole. He gave a leap and in he went—sticks, dirt, bait, and all. He picked himself up, rubbed sand out of his eyes, then began to jump, trying to get out. It was no use. He sent up a doleful howl.

He had stopped for breath when a Bear came along. "What are you howling for?" he asked. The Coyote cried out: "Broadfoot, lucky fellow! Did you hear me singing? I am the happiest creature on the face of the earth."

"What about? I shouldn't think you were happy, judging from your howling."

Said Coyote, "I was singing for joy. I came along this evening and by accident fell into this hole. And what do you suppose I found down here? Green corn, meat, sweet stuff, and everything a corn-eater could wish for. I need someone to enjoy the meal with me. Jump in: it isn't very deep."

So the old Bear jumped in. Coyote lay back, slapped his thighs, and laughed and laughed. "Now, get out if you can," said he to the Bear. "You and I are in a pretty mess. I fell in here by accident, but I would give my teeth and eyes to get out!"

The Bear came very near eating him up, but Coyote whispered something in his ear. "Good!" yelled the Bear. "Ha! Ha! Excellent idea! Let us sing together. Let them come!"

So they laughed, sang, and feasted until they attracted all the corn-pests. "Keep away, my friends," cried out Coyote. "We got here first."

"Can't I come?" cried out one after another.

"Well, yes—no—there may not be enough for you all."

"Come on though; come on! Who cares?" cried the Bear.

They rushed in so fast that the pit was almost full before they knew their predicament. The Coyote laughed, shuffled around, and climbed up over his grandfather Bear. He scrambled through the

others, which were snarling and biting each other, skipped over their backs, out of the hole, and ran away laughing.

The next morning the young man came down to the cornfield. Drawing near the pit, he heard a tremendous racket and saw it was half filled with pests. "My friends," cried the young man. "You must be cold; I'll warm you up." He gathered dry wood and threw it into the pit. He lit the wood and burned the rascals up. He noticed Coyote was not there.

He went back to the girl and reported what he had done. She was so pleased she hardly knew how to express it, but she asked him, "Are you sure they were all there?"

"All except Coyote," said the young man. "Somehow he got out or didn't get in."

"Who cares for Coyote?" said the girl. "I would rather marry a man with ingenuity than have all the Coyotes in the world to kill."

She accepted this ugly but ingenious young man. Ever since, pretty girls care little how their husbands look, but they like to have them able to think and guess at a way of getting along.

Thus it was in the days of the ancients. Coyote got out of the trap that was set for him by the ugly young man. That is the reason why Coyotes are more abundant than any other corn-pests in the land, and do what you will, they will get away with some of your corn, anyhow.

Inspired by ancient Paquimé ceramics, Mata Ortiz potter Andrés Villalba created this modern effigy pot.

Contemporary Navajo rug designed by Damian Jim and woven by Anita Hathale.

WILE E. COYOTE AND THE KITSCH MYSTIQUE

The ultimate modern Coyote myth came to us in celluloid.

Some of our strongest impressions of coyotes don't come from real coyotes. They come from the genius of animator Chuck Jones, who created the cartoon characters Wile E. Coyote and Road Runner in 1949. Whatever Coyote did, he never stopped getting viewer sympathy during his escapades: trying to catch Road Runner or Bugs Bunny, using Acme explosives he never seemed to pay for, or stealing sheep—no matter. Perhaps we see something of ourselves in his confidence and willingness to attempt a task—and in that last moment of knowledge, just before his efforts fail. Wile E. appeared in every *Road Runner* cartoon until the series ended in 1966.

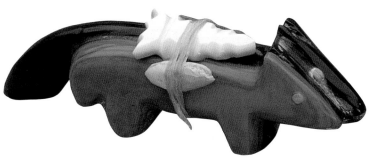

A "double coyotes" Zuni fetish by Aaron and Thelma Sheche, carved from a single piece of serpentine.

Reruns of Wile E. and his antics are still popular today, and we've embraced more that just his cartoon character in our everyday lives. The coyote shows up in brand names for fiery liquor, the names of athletic teams, votive candleholders, cookies, and more. We've got "coyote culture."

We've also done our best to make them endearing. In curio shops and stores throughout the West, you'll find items depicting this remarkable canid, usually at the edge of a cliff or situated among cactus, silhouetted against the moon in mid-howl. On potholders, refrigerator magnets, ashtrays, stuffed toys, and vases, Coyote is there—often wearing a bandanna.

What is this fascination humans have with coyotes? Is it that Coyote, the character, symbolizes all the things we wish we could be? Native Americans place Coyote in creation tales. He's also an outlaw, prankster, and thief, the ultimate individual who never conforms. He is always looking for new ways of doing things. Coyote represents the human condition and can never leave anything alone.

And perhaps he does like to howl at the moon—just as we wish *we* could.

Tularosa Black-on-white pitcher with a coyote or dog handle (A.D. 1100–1350, east-central New Mexico and west-central Arizona area).

"SONGDOG" ENCOUNTERS

You may never see them: night choruses may be the only evidence that coyotes live nearby. Suburban and urban environments provide tantalizing opportunities for coyote occupation: free food from trash containers and places to hole up, including parks, vacant lots, easements—any undisturbed areas. When coyotes become urbanized, human encounters with them are inevitable.

SOME PRACTICAL TIPS

DON'T FEED THEM! Encouraging coyotes with food handouts is tempting a normally cautious, wild predator to become a demanding one: they expect food—not a pat on the head! Though there are very few reports of coyote attacks on humans, almost all involved coyotes that were habituated and associated "people encounters" with potential food sources. Rabies can also be a threat among coyote populations, although no major outbreak of rabies in North American coyotes has been reported for more than sixty years. *Canis latrans* seem to show surprising resistance to rabies, unlike their fox kin.

KEEP GARBAGE IN HIGH-QUALITY GARBAGE CONTAINERS that latch securely. Coyotes have sharp teeth, strong jaws, and determination: they've been known to gnaw on old tire chunks when pressed for a meal, so the scent of chicken, fish, or leftover pet food wafting from your trash container is particularly tempting. Wrap food scraps tightly before disposing of them.

DON'T FEED PETS OUTDOORS OR LEAVE PET FOOD OUTSIDE where coyotes might be tempted. Coyotes—and many other wild critters—find ways to scale an eight-foot fence or wall with ease.

KEEP PETS INSIDE AT NIGHT. A free-roaming cat or small dog is fair game for coyotes. Though there isn't evidence that urbanized coyotes specialize in preying upon domestic pets, the risk exists. Keeping "prey-sized" pets inside a predator-proof enclosure—especially at night—offers the best protection.

VACCINATE YOUR PETS against rabies and distemper. If you see a coyote that seems disoriented, sick, or injured, stay away from the animal, and contact your local animal-control agency.

COYOTES DO NOT BECOME PETS. Coyotes are intrinsically wild. Any attempt to restrain or enclose them results in frustrating disappointment. If you "find" a coyote puppy and try to raise it, it doesn't lose its desire to be free—or any of its natural predator skills.

COYOTE COMPETITORS

BOBCATS An adult wild bobcat weighs in at twenty to thirty pounds, almost the same as a coyote. Like coyotes, bobcats are opportunistic omnivores. They adapt well to urban environments and share all habitats with coyotes where their territories overlap.

BADGERS This thirty- to forty-pound critter is a member of the weasel family. A tireless burrower, it shares the coyote's taste for small rodents. In fact, coyotes and badgers have a "hunting" relationship—unusual among competing predators.

FOXES Foxes are smaller than coyotes: kit foxes weigh about four to five pounds, while gray and red foxes average ten pounds. Gray foxes also climb trees well, seeking out birds' nests, fruit, or nuts, and they will sleep on shaded branches.

Digging for water.

MOUNTAIN LIONS This shy feline predator is known by more names than any other North American mammal: forty-two in English alone. An adult mountain lion weighs more than two hundred pounds. It competes with coyotes for food resources but prefers larger prey, such as deer and javelina.

OWLS Nighttime hunters, almost all owl species compete with coyotes for prey. Great-horned and barn owls take larger meals such as packrats, quail, and doves. Pint-sized screech owls and even tiny elf owls eat mice, voles, other small rodents, insects, and arthropods.

HAWKS AND EAGLES Hawks and eagles hunt during daylight hours and prey upon rodents, rabbits, and birds. Their hunting schedule overlaps with coyotes' at dawn and dusk. Red-tailed, Harris's, and Cooper's hawks are chief coyote competitors in the bird world, especially in suburban and urban areas. Golden and bald eagles also go after potential coyote prey.

Canis latrans among sandhill cranes, Bosque del Apache National Wildlife Refuge, New Mexico.

║ A RELATIONSHIP EVERLASTING ║

A strange, enduring bond exists between humans and canids of all species. During the long course of their evolution, some of these remarkable predators chose to live in our company as dogs: devoted servants and beloved companions.

The coyote chose freedom, despite the odds.

We admire the coyote's resiliency of spirit, often sung out in a ghostly chorus, whether in the desert Southwest, echoing over the waters off the Elizabeth Islands south of Cape Cod, in the boroughs of New York City, or the tropics of Guatemala.

WHERE YOU MIGHT SEE COYOTES

AT THE ZOO

Alameda Park Zoo, Alamogordo, NM

Amarillo Zoo, Amarillo, TX

Arizona-Sonora Desert Museum, Tucson, AZ

Bronx Zoo, Bronx, NY

Coyote Point Museum, San Mateo, CA

Dakota Zoo, Bismarck, ND

Fort Worth Zoological Park, Ft. Worth, TX

Great Plains Zoo, Sioux Falls, SD

The Living Desert Zoo and Gardens, Palm Desert, CA

Los Angeles Zoo and Botanical Gardens, Los Angeles, CA

Phoenix Zoo, Phoenix, AZ

Smithsonian National Zoological Park, Washington, D.C.

Southern Nevada Zoological Park, Las Vegas, NV

Willow Park Zoo, Logan, UT

Zoo New England/Franklin Park Zoo, Boston, MA

IN THE WILD

Coyotes are also often seen in state and national parks throughout the United States, including:

Anza-Borrego Desert State Park, Borrego Springs, CA

Big Bend National Park, TX

Bosque del Apache National Wildlife Refuge, NM

Chiricahua National Monument, AZ

Grand Canyon National Park, AZ

Organ Pipe Cactus National Monument, AZ

Petrified Forest National Park, AZ

Sabino Canyon Recreation Area, Tucson, AZ

Saguaro National Park, Tucson, AZ

Yellowstone National Park, WY

Yosemite National Park, CA

SUGGESTED READING

Cushing, Frank Hamilton. *Zuni Coyote Tales.* Tucson, Arizona: University of Arizona Press, 1998.

Hadidian, John, Guy R. Hodge, and John W. Grandy (editors). *Wild Neighbors: The Humane Approach to Living with Wildlife.* Golden, Colorado: Fulcrum Publishing, 1997.

Meinzer, Wyman. *Coyote.* Lubbock, Texas: Texas Tech University Press, 1995.

RECOMMENDED WEBSITES

www.desertusa.com/june96/du_cycot.html
www.junglewalk.com
www.nationalgeographic.com/kids/creature_feature/0005/coyote.html
www.twinrocks.com/stateartist/legends.html

PHOTOGRAPHY © AS FOLLOWS: